In the Year 1986

By

Kerry Butters.

In the Year 1986

Millennium:	2nd millennium
Centuries:	19th century – **20th century** – 21st century
Decades:	1950s 1960s 1970s – **1980s** – 1990s 2000s 2010s
Years:	1983 1984 1985 – **1986** – 1987 1988 1989

Disintegration of the Space Shuttle *Challenger*, January 28, 1986

1986 (MCMLXXXVI) was a common year starting on Wednesday (dominical letter E) of the Gregorian calendar, the 1986th year of the Common Era (CE) and *Anno Domini* (AD) designations, the 986th year of the 2nd millennium, the 86th year of the 20th century, and the 7th year of the 1980s decade. The year 1986 was designated as the **International Year of Peace** by the United Nations.

Contents

- 1 Events
- 2 Births
- 3 Deaths
- 4 Nobel Prizes
- In the news

Events

January

- January 1
    - Spain and Portugal enter the *European Community*, which later becomes the European Union.
    - Aruba gains increases autonomy from the Netherlands and is separated from the Netherlands Antilles.
    - The Province of Flevoland is established in the Netherlands.
    - UNIDO becomes a specialised agency of the United Nations.
    - In Northern Ireland as part of The Troubles, James McCandless (39) and Michael Williams (24), both Protestant members of the Royal Ulster Constabulary, are killed by a Provisional Irish Republican Army remote controlled bomb hidden in a litter bin and detonated when their foot patrol passes at Thomas Street, Armagh.

- January 9 – After losing a patent battle with Polaroid, Kodak leaves the instant camera business.
- January 11 – The Gateway Bridge in Brisbane, Australia, at this time the world's longest prestressed concrete free-cantilever bridge, is opened.
- January 12 – STS-61-C: Space Shuttle *Columbia* is launched with the first Hispanic American astronaut, Dr. Franklin Chang Díaz.
- January 13–24 – South Yemen Civil War.
- January 19 – The first PC virus, Brain, starts to spread.
- January 20 – The United Kingdom and France announce plans to construct the Channel Tunnel.
- January 24 – The Voyager 2 space probe makes its first encounter with Uranus.
- January 25 – Yoweri Museveni's National Resistance Army Rebel group takes over Uganda after leading a 5-year guerrilla war in which up to half a million people are believed to have been killed. They will later use January 26 as the official date to avoid a coincidence of dates with Dictator Idi Amin's 1971 coup.
- January 26 – Super Bowl XX was an American football game between the National Football Conference (NFC) champion Chicago Bears and the American Football Conference (AFC) champion New England Patriots to decide the National Football League (NFL) champion for the 1985 season. The Bears defeated the Patriots by the score of 46–10, capturing their first NFL championship since 1963, three years prior to the birth of the Super Bowl. Super Bowl XX was played on January 26, 1986 at the Louisiana Superdome in New Orleans, Louisiana.

- January 28 – Space Shuttle *Challenger* disaster – STS-51-L: Space Shuttle *Challenger* disintegrates 73 seconds after launch from the United States, killing the crew of 7 astronauts, including schoolteacher Christa McAuliffe.
- January 29 – Yoweri Museveni is sworn in as President of Uganda.

February

- February 3 – Pixar Animation Studios are opened in California.
- February 7 – President Jean-Claude Duvalier ("Baby Doc") flees Haiti, ending 28 years of family rule.
- February 9 – Halley's Comet reaches its perihelion, the closest point to the Sun, during its second visit to the solar system in the 20th century (the first was in 1910).
- February 11 – Human rights activist Natan Sharansky is released by the Soviet Union and leaves the country.
- February 15 – The Beechcraft Starship makes its maiden flight.
- February 16
  - The Soviet liner MS *Mikhail Lermontov* sinks in the Marlborough Sounds, New Zealand.
  - Ouadi Doum air raid: The French Air Force raids the Libyan Ouadi Doum airbase in northern Chad.
- February 17 – The Single European Act is signed.
- February 19
  - The Soviet Union launches the *Mir* space station.
  - The United States Senate approves a treaty outlawing genocide.

- February 21 – Nintendo releases the first game in the Zelda series, *The Legend of Zelda*, in Japan on the Famicom.
- February 22 – People Power Revolution begins in the Philippines to remove President Ferdinand Marcos from office.
- February 25
    - The 27th Congress of the Communist Party of the Soviet Union opens in Moscow. The General Secretary Mikhail Gorbachev introduces the keywords of his mandate to the audience: Glasnost and Perestroika.
    - People Power Revolution: President Ferdinand Marcos of the Philippines goes into exile in Hawaii after 20 years of rule; Corazon Aquino becomes the first Filipino woman president, first as an interim president. Salvador Laurel becomes her Vice President.
    - Egyptian military police, protesting against bad salaries, enter 4 luxury hotels near the pyramids, set fire to them and loot them.
- February 27 – The United States Senate allows its debates to be televised on a trial basis.
- February 28 – Assassination of Olof Palme: Swedish Prime Minister Olof Palme is assassinated on his way home from the cinema.

March

- March 1 – Olof Palme`s deputy Ingvar Carlsson becomes acting Prime Minister of Sweden. He is elected Prime Minister by the Swedish Riksdag on March 15 .

- March 3 – The first paper is published describing the atomic force microscope invented the previous year by Gerd Binnig, Calvin Quate and Christopher Berger.
- March 4 – The *Today* national tabloid newspaper is launched in the United Kingdom, pioneering the use of computer photosetting and full-colour offset printing, at a time when British national newspapers still use Linotype machines and letterpress printing.
- March 8 – The Japanese Suisei probe flies by Halley's Comet, studying its UV hydrogen corona and solar wind.
- March 9 – United States Navy divers find the largely intact but heavily damaged crew compartment of the Space Shuttle *Challenger*; the bodies of all seven astronauts are still inside.
- March 13 – In a Black Sea incident, American cruiser USS *Yorktown* and the destroyer USS *Caron*, claiming the right of innocent passage, enter the Soviet territorial waters near the southern Crimean Peninsula.
- March 14 – Microsoft Corporation holds its initial public offering of stock shares.
- March 15 – Collapse of the Hotel New World: The six-story Lian Yak Building (1971) in Singapore, housing the Hotel New World, collapses in less than a minute due to structural failure, perhaps caused by a gas explosion, trapping 50 people and killing 33 of them.
- March 25 – The 58th Academy Awards are held in Los Angeles, with *Out of Africa* winning Best Picture.
- March 26 – An article in *The New York Times* charges that Kurt Waldheim, former United Nations Secretary-General and candidate for president of Austria, may have been involved in Nazi war crimes during World War II.

- March 27 – Russell Street Bombing: A car bomb explodes at Russell Street Police Headquarters in Russell Street, Melbourne, killing a police constable, the first Australian policewoman to be killed in the line of duty.
- March 31
  - A fire causes extensive damage at Hampton Court Palace in Surrey, England.
  - Mexicana Flight 940 crashes near Maravatío, Mexico, killing 167.

April

- April 1 – Sector Kanda: Communist Party of Nepal (Mashal) cadres attack a number of police stations in Kathmandu, seeking to incite a popular rebellion.
- April 2 – A bomb explodes on a Trans World Airlines flight from Rome to Athens, killing 4 people.
- April 3 – The British children's TV show *The Raggy Dolls* is released on ITV in the UK.
- April 5
  - 1986 Berlin discotheque bombing: The West Berlin discothèque *La Belle*, a known hangout for United States soldiers, is bombed, killing 3 and injuring 230; Libya is held responsible.
  - Jean Michel Jarre plays Rendez-vous_Houston concert in Houston, Texas.
- April 13 – Pope John Paul II officially visits the Great Synagogue of Rome, the first time a modern Pope has visited a synagogue.

- April 13 – The first child born to a non-related surrogate mother is born.
- April 14 – Hailstones weighing 1 kg (2.2 lb) fall on the Gopalganj district of Bangladesh, killing 92.
- April 15 – Operation El Dorado Canyon: At least 15 people die after United States planes bomb targets in the Libyan capital, Tripoli, and the Benghazi region.
- April 17
    - John McCarthy is kidnapped in Beirut (released in August 1991) – 3 others are found dead; Revolutionary Cells claims responsibility in retaliation for the U.S. bombing of Libya.
    - The Hindawi affair begins when an Irishwoman is found unknowingly carrying explosives onto an El Al flight from London to Tel Aviv.
- April 21 – Geraldo Rivera opens Al Capone's secret vault on *The Mystery of Al Capone's Vaults*, discovering only a bottle of moonshine.
- April 26 – Chernobyl disaster: A mishandled safety test at the Chernobyl Nuclear Power Plant in Pripyat, Ukrainian SSR, Soviet Union "killed at least 4056 people and damaged almost $7 billion of property" Radioactive fallout from the accident is concentrated near Belarus, Ukraine and Russia and at least 350,000 people are forcibly resettled away from these areas. After the accident, "traces of radioactive deposits unique to Chernobyl were found in nearly every country in the northern hemisphere".
- April 27 – "Captain Midnight" interrupts the HBO satellite feed.

- April 29 – The Diamond Jubilee of Hirohito is held at the Kokugikan in Tokyo.

May

- May 2
  - Expo 86, the 1986 World Exposition on Transportation and Communication, a World's fair, opens in Vancouver, British Columbia, Canada.
  - The physical game show *Takeshi's Castle* first airs on the Tokyo Broadcasting System.
- May 3 – Sandra Kim from Belgium wins the Eurovision Song Contest in Bergen, Norway with her song *J'aime la vie*.
- May 8 – Óscar Arias is inaugurated into his first term as President of Costa Rica.
- May 9 – *Short Circuit* starring Fisher Stevens is released.
- May 12 – NBC debuts the current well-known peacock as seen in the NBC 60th Anniversary Celebration.
- May 16 – The Seville Statement on Violence is adopted by an international meeting of scientists, convened by the Spanish National Commission for UNESCO, in Seville, Spain.
- May 19 – The Firearm Owners Protection Act is enacted.
- May 23 – Somali President Siad Barre is injured in a car accident in Mogadishu and taken to Saudi Arabia for treatment. Somali opposition groups see this as an opportunity to try and remove Barre setting in stage the Somali Civil War.
- May 24 – The Montreal Canadiens win their 23rd Stanley Cup In Calgary against the Flames.
- May 25

- *Hands Across America*: At least 5,000,000 people form a human chain from New York City to Long Beach, California, to raise money to fight hunger and homelessness.
  - The Bangladeshi double decked ferry *Shamia* capsizes in the Meghna River, southern Barisal, Bangladesh, killing at least 600.
- May 27 – The game credited as setting the template for role-playing video games, *Dragon Quest*, is released in Japan.
- May 28 – Pingu premieres in Switzerland.
- May 31 – The 1986 FIFA World Cup begins in Mexico.

June

- June – Construction of the Oosterscheldekering, the world's largest openable storm surge flood barrier, is completed in the Netherlands.
- June 4 – Jonathan Pollard pleads guilty to espionage for selling top secret United States military intelligence to Israel.
- June 8 – Former United Nations Secretary-General Kurt Waldheim is elected president of Austria.
- June 9 – The Rogers Commission releases its report on the Space Shuttle *Challenger* disaster.
- June 12 – South Africa declares a nationwide state of emergency.
- June 19 – American college basketball player Len Bias suffers a fatal cardiac arrhythmia from a cocaine overdose, less than 48 hours after being selected 2nd overall by the Boston Celtics in the 1986 NBA draft.

- June 22 – In one of the most famous FIFA World Cup matches, Argentinian football player Diego Maradona scores one handball goal (nicknamed the "Hand of God") and then dribbles past the entire English football team to score a second goal (nicknamed "The Goal of the Century") with Argentina winning 2-1 against England.
- June 23 – Eric Thomas develops LISTSERV, the first email list management software.
- June 24 – The Dominican Republic recognizes the Sahrawi Arab Democratic Republic.
- June 29 – Argentina defeats West Germany 3–2 to win the 1986 FIFA World Cup in Mexico City.

July

- July 1 – CSX Transportation is established.
- July 5 – The Statue of Liberty is reopened to the public after an extensive refurbishment.
- July 5 – 20 – The Goodwill Games are held in Moscow.
- July 7 – Australian drug smugglers Kevin Barlow and Brian Chambers are executed in Malaysia.
- July 12 – The New Zealand Homosexual Law Reform Act decriminalises consensual sex between men from the age of 16.
- July 22 – In the Philippines, ABS-CBN Radio launches DZMM at 630 kHz on AM Band.
- July 23 – In London, Prince Andrew, Duke of York marries Sarah Ferguson at Westminster Abbey.
- July 27 – Greg LeMond wins the Tour de France.

- July 28 – Estate agent Suzy Lamplugh vanishes after a meeting in London.

August

- August 2 – The first film produced by Studio Ghibli, *Castle in the Sky* directed by Hayao Miyazaki is released in Japan.
- August 6
  - A low-pressure system moving from South Australia and redeveloping off the New South Wales coast dumps a record 328 millimetres (12.9 in) of rain in a day on Sydney.
  - In Louisville, Kentucky, William J. Schroeder, the second artificial heart recipient, dies after 620 days.
  - Australian Democrats leader Don Chipp retires from federal parliament and is succeeded by Janine Haines, the first woman to lead a political party in Australia.
- August 19 – Two weeks after it was stolen, the Picasso painting *Weeping Woman* is found in a locker at the Spencer Street Station in Melbourne, Australia.
- August 20 – In Edmond, Oklahoma, United States Postal Service employee Patrick Sherrill guns down 14 of his co-workers before committing suicide.
- August 21 – The Lake Nyos disaster, a limnic eruption, occurs in Cameroon, killing nearly 2,000 people.
- August 31
  - The Soviet passenger liner SS *Admiral Nakhimov* collides with the bulk carrier *Pyotr Vasev* in the Black Sea and sinks almost immediately, killing 398.

- Aeroméxico Flight 498, a Douglas DC-9, collides with a Piper PA-28 over Cerritos, California, killing 67 on both aircraft and 15 on the ground.
- The cargo ship *Khian Sea* departs from the docks of Philadelphia, carrying 14,000 tons of toxic waste. It wanders the seas for the next 16 months trying to find a place to dump its cargo. The waste is later dumped in Haiti.

September

- September 1 – Jordan University of Science and Technology is established in Jordan.
- September 4 – Eusko Alkartasuna, the Basque Social Democratic Party, is created in Vitoria-Gasteiz.
- September 5 – Pan Am Flight 73, with 358 people on board, is hijacked at Karachi International Airport by four Abu Nidal terrorists.
- September 6
  - The Big Mac Index is introduced in *The Economist* newspaper as a semi-humorous international measure of purchasing power parity.
  - In Istanbul, two Abu Nidal terrorists kill 22 and wound 6 inside the Neve Shalom Synagogue during Shabbat services.
- September 7
  - Desmond Tutu becomes the first black Anglican Church bishop in South Africa.

- Chilean dictator Augusto Pinochet survives an assassination attempt by the FPMR; 5 of his bodyguards are killed.
- September 8 – *The Oprah Winfrey Show* premieres in syndication.
- September 13 – A magnitude 6.0 earthquake rocks the city of Kalamata in southern Greece, killing 20 people, injuring 80 and completely destroying one-fifth of the city.
- September 28 – Democratic Progressive Party founded, that is Tangwai movement in new generation to challenge Kuomintang in Taiwan's one-party politics.

October

- October 1 – U.S. President Ronald Reagan signs the Goldwater–Nichols Act into law, making official the largest reorganization of the United States Department of Defense since the Air Force was made a separate branch of service in 1947.
- October 3 – TASCC, a superconducting cyclotron, officially opens at Chalk River Laboratories.
- October 9
  - United States District Court Judge Harry E. Claiborne becomes the fifth federal official to be removed from office through impeachment.
  - News Corporation completes its acquisition of the Metromedia group of companies, thereby launching the Fox Broadcasting Company.

- *The Phantom of the Opera*, the longest running Broadway show in history, opens at Her Majesty's Theatre in London.
- October 10 – The 5.7 Mw San Salvador earthquake shook San Salvador, El Salvador with a maximum Mercalli intensity of IX (Violent). Up to 1,500 people were killed.
- October 11 – 12 – Cold War: Ronald Reagan and Soviet leader Mikhail Gorbachev meet in Reykjavík, Iceland, to continue discussions about scaling back their intermediate missile arsenals in Europe (the talks break down in failure).
- October 12 – Elizabeth II and The Duke of Edinburgh visit the People's Republic of China.
- October 16 – The International Olympic Committee chooses Albertville, France to be the host city of the 1992 Winter Olympics and Barcelona, Spain to be the host city of the 1992 Summer Olympics. The IOC also announces that the summer and winter games will separate with the winter games on every even, common year; and the summer games on every even, leap year starting from 1992.
- October 19 – Mozambican president Samora Machel's plane crashes in South Africa.
- October 21 – The Marshall Islands become an associated state under the Compact of Free Association.
- October 22 – In New York City, WNBC Radio's traffic helicopter crashes into the Hudson River, killing traffic reporter Jane Dornacker. The last words heard on-the-air are Dornacker's screams of terror, "Hit the water! Hit the water! Hit the water!"

- October 24 – Lambda Sigma Gamma Sorority Inc. is founded at Sacramento State by Linda V. Fuentes and 26 Founding Mothers.
- October 26 – Bus deregulation goes into effect in the United Kingdom, except Greater London and Northern Ireland.
- October 27
  - The International World Day of Prayer is held in Assisi, Italy.
  - World Series: The New York Mets defeat the Boston Red Sox in 7 games. This is the second world series title in the Mets franchise. It is also remembered for Game 6, when Bill Buckner lets a routine ground ball hit by Mookie Wilson roll through his legs, letting the Mets win and pull even with the Red Sox in the series.
  - The Big Bang in the London Stock Exchange abolishes fixed commission charges, paving the way for electronic trading.
- October 28
  - The centennial of the Statue of Liberty's dedication is celebrated in New York Harbor.
  - In London, Jeremy Bamber is found guilty of the murder of his adoptive parents, sister and twin nephews, and sentenced to life imprisonment, with a recommendation by the trial judge that he should serve at least 25 years before being considered for parole.
- October 29 – British Prime Minister Margaret Thatcher officially opens the M25 Motorway, which encircles Greater London, in a ceremony on the carriageway near Potters Bar. It became Europe's second longest orbital road upon

completion, and provides the first and only full bypass of London.

November

- November 1
    - Queensland, Australia: Joh Bjelke-Petersen wins his final election as Premier of Queensland with 38.6% of the vote. He resigns on December 1, 1987 following revelations of his involvement with corruption released in the Fitzgerald Inquiry.
    - Sandoz chemical spill: a major environmental disaster near Basel, Switzerland, pollutes the Rhine.
- November 3
    - Iran–Contra affair: The Lebanese magazine *Ash-Shiraa* reports that the United States has been selling weapons to Iran in secret, in order to secure the release of 7 American hostages held by pro-Iranian groups in Lebanon.
    - Commonwealth of the Northern Mariana Islands (CNMI) in Political Union with the United States. The CNMI Government adopted its own constitution in 1977, and the constitutional government took office in January 1978. The Covenant was fully implemented November 3, 1986, pursuant to Presidential Proclamation no. 5564, which conferred United States citizenship on legally qualified CNMI residents.
- November 4 – Democrats regain control of the United States Senate for the first time in 6 years. In California, Chief Justice Rose Bird and two colleagues are removed by voters from

the Supreme Court of California for opposing capital punishment.

- November 6 – Sumburgh disaster: A British International Helicopters Boeing 234LR Chinook crashes 2.5 miles east of Sumburgh Airport, killing 45 people (the deadliest civilian helicopter crash on record).
- November 11 – Sperry Rand and Burroughs merge to form Unisys, becoming the second largest computer company.
- November 12 – Australian singer John Farnham releases the album *Whispering Jack*, which becomes the highest selling album in Australia's history.
- November 18 – Greater Manchester Police announce that they will search for the bodies of 2 missing children (who both vanished more than 20 years ago) after the Moors murderers Ian Brady and Myra Hindley confess to 2 more murders.
- November 21 – Iran-Contra Affair: National Security Council member Oliver North and his secretary, Fawn Hall, start shredding documents implicating them in selling weapons to Iran and channeling the proceeds to help fund the Contra rebels in Nicaragua.
- November 22 – Mike Tyson wins his first world boxing title by defeating Trevor Berbick in Las Vegas.
- November 25 – Iran–Contra affair: U.S. Attorney General Edwin Meese announces that profits from covert weapons sales to Iran were illegally diverted to the anti-communist Contra rebels in Nicaragua.
- November 26 – Iran–Contra affair: U.S. President Ronald Reagan announces that on December 1 former Senator John Tower, former Secretary of State Edmund Muskie, and

former National Security Adviser Brent Scowcroft will serve as members of the Special Review Board looking into the scandal (they became known as the Tower Commission). Reagan denies involvement in the scandal.

December

- December 7 – A magnitude 5.7 earthquake destroys most of the Bulgarian town of Strajica, killing 2 people.
- December 14 – Rutan Voyager, an experimental aircraft designed by Burt Rutan and piloted by Dick Rutan and Jeana Yeager, begins its flight around the world.
- December 19 – Soviet dissident Andrei Sakharov is permitted to return to Moscow after six years of internal exile.
- December 20 – Three African Americans are assaulted by a group of white teens in the Howard Beach neighborhood of Queens, New York. One of the victims, Michael Griffith, is run over and killed by a motorist while attempting to flee the attackers.
- December 23 – Voyager completes the first nonstop circumnavigation of the earth by air without refueling in 9 days, 3 minutes and 44 seconds.
- December 26 – After 35 years on the airwaves and holding the title of longest-running non-news program on network television, NBC airs the final episode of daytime drama *Search for Tomorrow*.
- December 31 – A fire at the Dupont Plaza Hotel in San Juan, Puerto Rico, kills 97 and injures 140.

Date unknown

- The National Park Passport Stamps program begins.
- The Council on Competitiveness is founded.
- Average per capita income in Japan exceeds that in the United States.
- Matt Groening creates The Simpsons family.
- The first commercially available 3D printer is sold.
- Informal stock trading is done in Shenyang, China; the first of its kind in Red China.

Births

January

Colin Morgan

Zlata Ognevich

Deepika Padukone

Raviv Ullman

- January 1
  - Glen Davis, American basketball player
  - Colin Morgan, Northern Irish actor
  - Lee Sungmin, South Korean singer
- January 2
  - Nathan Cowen, New Zealand rower
  - Trombone Shorty, American jazz musician
- January 3 – Lloyd, American R&B recording artist
- January 4

- Katrina Halili, Filipina actress and commercial model
  - James Milner, English soccer player
  - Steve Slaton, American football player
  - Hsieh Su-wei, Taiwanese tennis player
- January 5
  - Teppei Koike, Japanese singer and actor
  - Deepika Padukone, Bollywood actress
- January 6
  - Petter Northug, Norwegian cross-country skier
  - Irina Shayk, Russian model
  - Alex Turner, English musician (Arctic Monkeys)
- January 8 – David Silva, Spanish footballer
- January 10
  - Chen Jin, Chinese badminton player
  - Kenneth Vermeer, Dutch footballer
- January 11
  - Daniela de Jesus Cosio, Mexican model
  - Kieron Richardson, English actor
- January 12 – Zlata Ognevich, Ukrainian singer
- January 13 – Joannie Rochette, Canadian figure skater
- January 14 – Yohan Cabaye, French footballer
- January 15 – Jessy Schram, American actress
- January 16 – Paula Pareto, Argentinian judoka
- January 17
  - Max Adler, American actor
  - Chloe Rose Lattanzi, Australian actress and singer
- January 18 – Marya Roxx, Estonian-born musician
- January 19 – Claudio Marchisio, Italian footballer
- January 20 – Genie Chuo, Taiwanese singer and actress
- January 21

- o Peyton Hillis, American football player
- o Sushant Singh Rajput, Indian actor
- January 22 – Daniel Smith, American actor (d. 2006)
- January 23
  - o José Enrique Sánchez, Spanish footballer
  - o Joseph Torrez, professional MMA fighter
- January 24
  - o Mischa Barton, British-American actress
  - o Raviv Ullman, Israeli-American actor
- January 26
  - o Gerald Green, American basketball player
  - o Matt Heafy, Japanese-American musician
  - o Jaejoong, South Korean singer
  - o Shantelle Malawski, Canadian professional wrestler
- January 28
  - o Jessica Ennis-Hill, British heptathlete
  - o Shruti Haasan, Indian actress and musician
- January 29 – Drew Tyler Bell, American actor and dancer
- January 31 – Yves Makabu-Makalambay, Belgian footballer

February

Lauren Conrad

Gemma Arterton

Dane DeHaan

Tiffany Thornton

Teresa Palmer

- February 1 – Lauren Conrad, American television personality and fashion designer
- February 2
  - Gemma Arterton, British actress

- Miwa Asao, Japanese beach volleyball player
  - Tiffany Vise, American figure skater
- February 5
  - Claudia Cruz, Dominican model and beauty queen
  - Madison Rayne, American professional wrestler
- February 6
  - Vedran Ćorluka, Croatian international footballer
  - Sofia Nizharadze, Georgian singer, actress and songwriter
  - Yunho, South Korean singer and actor
  - Dane DeHaan, American actor
- February 7 – Stephen Colletti, American actor and television personality
- February 8 – Charles Andrew Williams, American perpetrator of the Santana High School shootings
- February 10
  - Radamel Falcao, Colombian footballer
  - Yui Ichikawa, Japanese actress
- February 14
  - Tiffany Thornton, American actress
  - Aschwin Wildeboer, Spanish swimmer
- February 15
  - Valeri Bojinov, Bulgarian footballer
  - Amber Riley, American actress
  - Ami Koshimizu, Japanese voice actress
- February 18
  - Brenan Espartinez, Filipino singer and actor
  - Vika Jigulina, Romanian music producer, singer and DJ
  - Alessandra Mastronardi, Italian actress
- February 19

- o Marta (Vieira da Silva), Brazilian-born footballer
- o Björn Gustafsson, Swedish comedian
- o Ophelia Lovibond, English actress
- o Maria Mena, Norwegian singer
- February 21
  - o Prince Amedeo of Belgium, Archduke of Austria-Este, member of the Belgian Royal Family
  - o Charlotte Church, Welsh singer, actress and television presenter
- February 23
  - o Emerson da Conceição, Brazilian footballer
  - o Skylar Grey, American singer-songwriter
  - o Kazuya Kamenashi, Japanese singer-songwriter and actor (KAT-TUN and Shūji to Akira)
  - o Boipelo Makhothi, Lesotho swimmer
  - o Jerod Mayo, American football player
  - o Ola Svensson, Swedish singer-songwriter
- February 24 – Bryce Papenbrook, American voice actor, son of Bob Papenbrook
- February 25
  - o Justin Berfield, American actor
  - o James and Oliver Phelps, identical twin British actors
  - o Danny Saucedo (aka Danny), Swedish singer
- February 26
  - o Leila Lopes, Angolan Miss Universe 2011
  - o Teresa Palmer, Australian actress and model
  - o Crystal Kay, Japanese singer and actress

March

Jamie Bell

Alexandra Daddario

Lady Gaga

Mika Newton

- March 1 – Jonathan Spector, American soccer player
  - Ayumu Goromaru, Japanese rugby union player
- March 2 – Ethan Peck, American actor
- March 3 – Stacie Orrico, American singer
- March 4 – Margo Harshman, American actress
- March 5
  - Corey Brewer, American basketball player
  - Julie Henderson, American model
  - Mika Newton, Ukrainian singer and actress
  - Andrew Jenks, American filmmaker
  - Shikabala, Egyptian footballer
- March 6
  - Francisco Cervelli, American baseball player
  - Charlie Mulgrew, Scottish footballer
- March 8 – Princess Tsuguko of Takamado, a member of the Japanese Imperial Family
- March 9 – Brittany Snow, American actress
- March 11
  - Dario Cologna, Swiss cross-country skier
  - Mariko Shinoda, Japanese singer, actress, fashion model, and idol (AKB48)
- March 12 – Danny Jones, English musician
- March 13
  - Chiaki Kyan, Japanese gravure idol

- Kousuke Yonehara, Japanese singer (Run&Gun) and actor
- March 14 – Jamie Bell, British actor
- March 16
    - Alexandra Daddario, American actress and model
    - Ken Doane, American professional wrestler
    - T. J. Jordan, American basketball player
    - Daisuke Takahashi, Japanese figure skater
- March 17
    - Edin Džeko, Bosnian footballer
    - Olesya Rulin, Russian-born actress
- March 18 – Lykke Li, Swedish singer-songwriter.
- March 19 – Anne Vyalitsyna, Russian model
- March 21 – Scott Eastwood, American actor
- March 22 – Matt Bush, American actor
- March 23 – Brett Eldredge, American country music singer
- March 25
    - Marco Belinelli, Italian basketball player
    - Megan Gibson, American softball player
- March 26
    - Jonny Craig, Canadian singer and songwriter
    - Jessica Hart, Australian model
- March 27
    - SoCal Val, American professional wrestling personality
    - Manuel Neuer, German football goalkeeper
- March 28 – Lady Gaga (real name Stefani Germanotta), American singer-songwriter and record producer
- March 29 – Romina Oprandi, Italian tennis player
- March 30 – Sergio Ramos, Spanish footballer

April

Amber Heard

Amanda Bynes

- April 1
    - Kid Ink, American rapper, singer, and songwriter
    - Yurika Nakamura, Japanese long-distance runner
    - Hillary Scott, American singer/songwriter (Lady Antebellum)
- April 2 – Lee DeWyze, American singer/songwriter
- April 3
    - Amanda Bynes, American actress
    - Coleen Rooney, English media personality

- April 4 – Eunhyuk, South Korean singer and actor
- April 7 – Siwon, South Korean singer, actor and model
- April 8
  - Igor Akinfeev, Russian footballer
  - Cliff Avril, American football player
  - Félix Hernández, Venezuelan baseball player
  - Erika Sawajiri, Japanese actress, singer, and model
- April 9 – Leighton Meester, American actress
- April 10
  - Sam Attwater, English actor
  - Fernando Gago, Argentine footballer
  - Vincent Kompany, Belgian footballer
- April 11 – Stephanie Pratt, American television personality
- April 16 – Shinji Okazaki, Japanese football player
- April 18 – Maurice Edu, American footballer
- April 19 – Candace Parker, American basketball player
- April 20
  - Pablo Martín, Spanish golfer
  - Cameron Duncan, New Zealand director and writer (d. 2003)
- April 22
  - Viktor Fayzulin, Russian footballer
  - Amber Heard, American actress
  - Marshawn Lynch, American football player
- April 23 – Jessica Stam, Canadian model
- April 24 – Tahyna Tozzi, Australian model, singer and actress
- April 27
  - Jenna-Louise Coleman, English actress
  - Dinara Safina, Russian tennis player

- April 28 – Jenna Ushkowitz, American stage and television actress and singer
- April 30 – Dianna Agron, American actress

May

Robert Pattinson

Alexander Rybak

Megan Fox

Seth Rollins

- May 2 – Emily Hart, American actress
- May 5 – Grace Wong, Hong Kong actress and beauty pageant contestant
- May 7 – Rianne ten Haken, Dutch model
- May 9 – Grace Gummer, American actress
- May 12 – Emily VanCamp, Canadian actress
- May 13
    - Robert Pattinson, English actor

- Alexander Rybak, Norwegian singer and violinist, Eurovision Song Contest 2009 winner
- Lena Dunham, American actress and producer
- May 14 – Alyosha, Ukrainian singer
- May 15 – Matías Fernández, Chilean footballer
- May 16
  - Megan Fox, American actress
  - Shamcey Supsup, Filipino beauty pageant contestant
  - Jacob Zachar, American actor
- May 17 – Tahj Mowry, American actor, dancer, and singer
- May 20 – Dexter Blackstock, English footballer
- May 21
  - Ricardo Lockette, American football player
  - Mario Mandžukić, Croatian footballer
- May 22 – Tatiana Volosozhar, Ukrainian figure skater
- May 23
  - Nico Colaluca, American footballer
  - Valentina Marchei, Italian figure skater
  - Jordan Zimmermann, American baseball player
- May 25 – Juri Ueno, Japanese actress
- May 26 – Àstrid Bergès-Frisbey, Spanish actress and model
- May 27 – Timo Descamps, Belgian actor and singer
- May 28
  - Joseph Cross, American actor
  - Charles N'Zogbia, French footballer
  - Britt McHenry, American sports reporter
  - Seth Rollins, American professional wrestler
- May 29 – Jaslene Gonzalez, Puerto Rican-American fashion model
- May 30 – Pasha Parfeni, Moldovan singer

- May 31
  - Brooke Castile, American figure skater
  - Robert Gesink, Dutch cyclist
  - Sopho Khalvashi, Georgian musician

June

Rafael Nadal

Shia LaBeouf

Kat Dennings

Måns Zelmerlöw

Drake Bell

- June 1
  - Moses Ndiema Masai, Kenyan runner
  - Dayana Mendoza, Miss Universe 2008
  - Chinedu Obasi, Nigerian footballer
  - Skream, English DJ and producer (Magnetic Man)
  - Ben Smith, New Zealand rugby player
- June 2
  - Todd Carney, Australian rugby player
  - Curtis Lofton, American football player
- June 3
  - Al Horford, Dominican basketball player
  - Brenden Jefferson, American actor
  - Alexandros Karageorgiou, Greek archer
  - Micah Kogo, Kenyan runner
  - Rafael Nadal, Spanish tennis player
  - Adrián Vallés, Spanish race car driver
  - Tomáš Verner, Czech Republic ice skater
- June 4
  - Oona Chaplin, Spanish-English actress and dancer
  - Fahriye Evcen, German-Turkish actress
  - Shane Kippel, Canadian actor
  - Shelly Woods, English wheelchair racer
  - Yoochun, South Korean musician and actor
- June 5
  - Christian Baracat, German rugby player
  - Dave Bolland, Canadian ice hockey player
  - Amanda Crew, Canadian actress
  - Vernon Gholston, American football player
- June 6
  - Bhavana, Indian actress

- o Kim Hyun-joong, South Korean actor, model and singer
- o Junichi Tazawa, Japanese-American baseball player
- June 11 – Shia LaBeouf, American actor
- June 12 – Cintia Dicker, Brazilian model
- June 13
  - o Kat Dennings, American actress
  - o DJ Snake, French DJ and producer
  - o Keisuke Honda, Japanese football player
  - o Ashley Olsen, American actress
  - o Mary-Kate Olsen, American actress
  - o Måns Zelmerlöw, Swedish pop singer and television presenter
- June 15 – Momoko Ueda, Japanese golfer
- June 18
  - o Richard Gasquet, French tennis player
  - o Richard Madden, Scottish actor
  - o Shusaku Nishikawa, Japanese footballer
  - o Crystal Renn, American model and author
- June 19 – Marvin Williams, American basketball player
- June 20 – Dreama Walker, American actress
- June 24
  - o Bojana Stamenov, Serbian singer
  - o Phil Hughes, American baseball player
- June 25 – Lee Ho-suk, South Korean short-track skater
- June 26 – Brittney Karbowski, American voice actress
- June 27
  - o Drake Bell, American actor and singer
  - o Sam Claflin, English actor
- June 28

- ○ Kellie Pickler, American singer
- ○ Shadia Simmons, Canadian actress
- June 29 – Edward Maya, Romanian musician
- June 30 – Victoria Crawford, American professional wrestler and model

July

Lindsay Lohan

Dan Smith

Hulk

- July 1
  - Agnes Monica, Indonesian singer
  - Casey Reinhardt, American model
- July 2 – Lindsay Lohan, American actress and singer
- July 4 – Takahisa Masuda, Japanese actor and singer
- July 5 – Adam Young, American singer-songwriter and multi-instrumentalist (Owl City)
- July 7 – Sevyn Streeter, American R&B singer and songwriter
- July 8
  - Renata Costa, Brazilian footballer
  - Jake McDorman, American film and television actor
- July 9
  - Caroline D'Amore, American model
  - Kiely Williams, American actress and singer
- July 12
  - Krystal Forscutt, Australian reality TV star
  - JP Pietersen, South African rugby player
- July 14 – Dan Smith, English singer-songwriter (Bastille)

- July 17
  - Dana, Korean singer, dancer and actress (TSZX)
  - Lacey Von Erich, professional wrestler
- July 18
  - Brando Eaton, American film and television actor
  - Travis Milne, Canadian actor
  - Kaitlin Riley, American actress
- July 24
  - Megan Park, Canadian actress and singer
  - Natalie Tran, Australian comedian
- July 25 – Hulk, Brazilian footballer
- July 26 – Monica Raymund, American actress
- July 28 – Alexandra Chando, American actress
- July 30 – Jung Chul-woon, South Korean football player
- July 31 – Evgeni Malkin, Russian hockey player

August

Usain Bolt

Armie Hammer

Lea Michele

- August 3
  - Charlotte Casiraghi, heir to the Monaco throne
  - Prince Louis of Luxembourg, Prince of Luxembourg
- August 4 – Oleg Ivanov, Russian footballer
- August 5 – Paula Creamer, American golfer
- August 6 – Bryan Young, Canadian ice hockey player
- August 7
  - Paul Biedermann, German swimmer

- Nancy Sumari, Tanzanian beauty queen and model, Miss World 2005
- August 11
  - Kaori Fukuhara, Japanese voice actress
  - Colby Rasmus, American baseball player
- August 14 – Nigel Boogaard, Australian footballer
- August 16
  - Yu Darvish, Japanese baseball player
  - Shawn Pyfrom, American actor
- August 17 – Tobias Schönenberg, German actor and photo model
- August 19 – Christina Perri, American singer-songwriter and musician
- August 21 – Usain Bolt, Jamaican sprinter
- August 22 – Keiko Kitagawa, Japanese actress
- August 26 – Big K.R.I.T., American rapper
- August 28
  - Armie Hammer, American actor
  - Gilad Shalit, Israeli soldier/hostage
  - Florence Welch, British singer
- August 29
  - Lauren Collins, Canadian actress
  - Lea Michele, American actress and singer
- August 30
  - Theo Hutchcraft, British pop musician
  - Ryan Ross, American guitarist (Panic! at the Disco)
- August 31 – Feng Tianwei, Singaporean Olympic table tennis player

September

Emmy Rossum

Lindsey Stirling

- September 1
  - Sidney Rice, former American football player
  - Shahar Tzuberi, Israeli windsurfer
- September 2
  - Moses Ndiema Kipsiro, Ugandan middle-distance runner
  - Stevan Faddy, Montenegrin singer
- September 3

- OMI, Jamaican-born singer
- Shaun White, American professional snowboarder
- September 6 – Raven Riley, American porn star
- September 8 – Jake Sandvig, American actor
- September 9 – José Aldo, WEC Featherweight Champion, the first UFC Featherweight Champion
- September 10 – Ryuji Kamiyama, Japanese vocalist (Run&Gun) and actor
- September 12
  - Yang Mi, Chinese actress and singer
  - Yuto Nagatomo, Japanese footballer
  - Emmy Rossum, American actress and singer
- September 14
  - Tinchy Stryder, Ghanaian musician
  - Ai Takahashi, Japanese singer
  - A.J. Trauth, American actor and musician
- September 15
  - Jenna McCorkell, British figure skater
  - Heidi Montag, American television personality
- September 16
  - Gordon Beckham, American baseball player
  - Ian Harding, American actor
  - Kyla Pratt, American actress
- September 18
  - Keeley Hazell, British model
  - Renaud Lavillenie, French pole vaulter
- September 19
  - Mandy Musgrave, American actress
  - Ilya Salmanzadeh, Swedish music producer
  - Peter Vack, American voice actor

- September 21 – Lindsey Stirling, American violinist, dancer, performance artist, and composer
- September 24 – Leah Dizon, American singer and model
- September 25 – Steve Forrest, American drummer
- September 26 – Ashley Leggat, Canadian actress
- September 27 – Natasha Thomas, Danish singer and songwriter
- September 28 – Andrés Guardado, Mexican footballer
- September 30 – Olivier Giroud, French footballer

October

Camilla Bello

Drake

- October 1 – Jurnee Smollett, American actress
- October 2
  - Camilla Belle, American actress

- Tom Hudson, British actor
- October 4 – Yuridia, Mexican singer
- October 5 – Novica Veličković, Serbian basketball player
- October 6
  - Tereza Kerndlová, Czech singer
  - Olivia Thirlby, American actress
- October 7 – Amber Stevens, American actress and model
- October 9 – Laure Manaudou, French swimmer
- October 10 – Nathan Jawai, Australian basketball player
- October 12 – Marcus T. Paulk, American actor
- October 13 – Gabriel Agbonlahor, English Footballer
- October 14
  - Wesley Matthews, American basketball player
  - Skyler Shaye, American actress
- October 15 – Lee Donghae, Korean singer (Super Junior)
- October 16 – Craig Pickering, British sprinter
- October 17 – Mohombi, Swedish-Congolese R&B singer-songwriter and dancer
- October 18 – Loukas Giorkas, Greek-Cypriot singer and model
- October 20 – Elyse Taylor, Australian model
- October 21
  - Tamerlan Tsarnaev, Russian-American terrorist responsible for the Boston Marathon bombings (d. 2013)
  - Christopher Uckermann, Mexican actor
- October 22
  - Kyle Gallner, American actor
  - Kara Lang, Canadian footballer
- October 23

- ○ Briana Evigan, American actress
- ○ Jessica Stroup, American actress and fashion model
- October 24 – Drake, Canadian actor and rapper
- October 26 – Emilia Clarke, British actress
- October 28 – Tamar Kaprelian, Armenian American musician and singer
- October 29 – Italia Ricci, Canadian actress
- October 30 – Thomas Morgenstern, Austrian ski jumper

November

Penn Badgley

Alexz Johnson

Josh Peck

Katie Cassidy

Jordan Farmar

- November 1 – Penn Badgley, American actor
- November 3 – Jasmine Trias, Filipino-American singer
- November 4 – Alexz Johnson, Canadian actress and singer
- November 5
  - BoA, Korean singer
  - Kasper Schmeichel, Danish footballer
  - Nodiko Tatishvili, Georgian singer
- November 10 – Josh Peck, American actor and director
- November 11
  - Greta Salóme, Icelandic singer and violinist
  - François Trinh-Duc, French rugby player
- November 12 – Evan Yo, Taiwanese singer-songwriter
- November 14 – Yuna, Malaysian singer, songwriter, and businesswoman
- November 15 – Sania Mirza, Indian tennis player
- November 17
  - Karmichael Hunt, Australian NRL player
  - Nani, Cape Verde-born Portuguese footballer
- November 18 – Georgia King, Scottish actress
- November 19 – Veronica Scott, American fashion designer
- November 20 – Lee Gye-deok, South Korean singer and activist
- November 22 – Oscar Pistorius, South African Paralympic runner
- November 24
  - Jimmy Graham, American football player
  - Pedro León, Spanish soccer player
  - Mohamed Massaquoi, American football player
  - Guðmundur Pétursson, Icelandic soccer player
- November 25

- Katie Cassidy, American singer and model
- Amber Hagerman, American murder victim and namesake for the AMBER Alert system (d. 1996)
- November 27 – Suresh Raina, Indian cricket player
- November 28 – Pamela Bianca Manalo, Filipina beauty queen and actress
- November 30
  - Boggie, Hungarian singer
  - Jordan Farmar, American basketball player

December

Amir Khan

Ellie Goulding

- December 1 – DeSean Jackson, American football player
- December 4 – Martell Webster, American basketball player
- December 7 – Corey Vidal, Canadian online video content provider and digital media consultant
- December 8
  - Amir Khan, British boxer
  - Kate Voegele, American singer/songwriter and actress
- December 11
  - Alex House, Canadian actor
  - Lee Peltier, English footballer
- December 15
  - Radosław Majewski, Polish footballer
  - Xiah, Korean singer (TVXQ)
- December 18 – Jery Sandoval, Colombian actress, model and singer
- December 19
  - Ryan Babel, Dutch footballer
  - Calvin Andrew, English footballer
- December 22 – Umar Farouk Abdulmutallab, Nigerian-born terrorist known as the "Underwear Bomber"
- December 24
  - Tim Elliott, American mixed martial artist
  - Satomi Ishihara, Japanese actress
  - Riyo Mori, Japanese Miss Universe 2007 winner
- December 26
  - Mew Azama, Japanese actress
  - Kit Harington, English actor
- December 27 – Jamaal Charles, American football player
- December 29 – Kim Ok-bin, South Korean actress and model
- December 30 – Ellie Goulding, British artist

Deaths

January

Phil Lynott

Donna Reed

Christa McAuliffe

- January 2 – Una Merkel, American actress (b. 1903)
- January 4

- Christopher Isherwood, English writer (b. 1904)
- Phil Lynott, Irish musician, lead singer and bassist of Thin Lizzy (b. 1949)
- January 7 – Juan Rulfo, Mexican writer (b. 1917)
- January 8 – Maria L. de Hernández, Mexican-American rights activist (b. 1896)
- January 10 – Jaroslav Seifert, Czech writer, Nobel Prize laureate (b. 1901)
- January 14 – Donna Reed, American actress (b. 1921)
- January 16 – Herbert W. Armstrong, founded the Worldwide Church of God (b. 1892)
- January 23 – Willard Van Dyke, American filmmaker and photographer (b. 1906)
- January 24
  - L. Ron Hubbard, American writer and founder of Scientology (b. 1911)
  - Gordon MacRae, American actor and singer (b. 1921)
- January 27 – Lilli Palmer, German actress (b. 1914)
- January 28
  - Joan Bennett, Cambridge literary scholar and critic (b. 1896)
  - Tatiana Botkina, daughter of Eugene Botkin (b. 1898)
  - William P. Murphy, Associate Justice (b. 1898)
  - Guang Qin, Buddhist monk and teacher (b. 1892)
  - In the *Challenger* disaster:
    - Gregory Jarvis, American astronaut (b. 1944)
    - Christa McAuliffe, American astronaut and teacher (b. 1948)
    - Ronald McNair, American astronaut (b. 1950)
    - Ellison Onizuka, American astronaut (b. 1946)

- Judith Resnik, American astronaut (b. 1949)
- Dick Scobee, American astronaut (b. 1939)
- Michael J. Smith, American astronaut (b. 1945)
- January 29 – Leif Erickson, American actor (b. 1911)

February

Olof Palme

Frank Herbert

- February 1 – Alva Myrdal, Swedish politician, diplomat, and writer, recipient of the Nobel Peace Prize (b. 1902)
- February 6 – Frederick Coutts, the 8th General of The Salvation Army (b. 1899)
- February 7 – Minoru Yamasaki, Japanese-American architect, designed the twin towers of the World Trade Center (b. 1912)
- February 8 – Sarah Isabella McElligott, New Zealand cook and fruit-stall holder (b. 1883)

- February 10 – Brian Aherne, British actor (b. 1902)
- February 11
  - Frank Herbert, American author (b. 1920)
  - Evelio Javier, Filipino politician, lawyer, and civil servant (b. 1942)
- February 14 – Edmund Rubbra, British composer (b. 1901)
- February 16 – Howard Da Silva, American actor (b. 1909)
- February 17
  - Jiddu Krishnamurti, Indian philosopher (b. 1895)
  - Red Ruffing, American baseball player (New York Yankees) and member of the MLB Hall of Fame (b. 1905)
- February 19 – Francisco Mignone, Brazilian classical music (b. 1897)
- February 21
  - Helen Hooven Santmyer, American writer (b. 1895)
  - Mart Stam, Dutch architect (b. 1899)
- February 24 – Tommy Douglas, Canadian politician and "Father of medicare" in Canada (b. 1904)
- February 27 – Jacques Plante, Canadian hockey player (b. 1929)
- February 28
  - Olof Palme, Swedish politician, Prime Minister of Sweden (b. 1927)
  - Thomas Williams, British politician (b. 1915)

March

Georgia O'Keeffe

Ray Milland

James Cagney

- March 4
  - Richard Manuel, Canadian musician (The Band) (b. 1943)
  - Howard Greenfield, American songwriter (b. 1936)
- March 6

- Adolph Caesar, American actor (b. 1933)
- Lewis Valentine, Welsh politician (b. 1893)
- Georgia O'Keeffe, American artist (b. 1887)
- Alexander Hollaender, radiation biology (b. 1898)
- March 10
  - Myron Cohen, American comedian (b. 1902)
  - Ray Milland, Welsh actor (b. 1907)
- March 17 – John Bagot Glubb, British soldier (b. 1897)
- March 18 – Bernard Malamud, American writer (b. 1914)
- March 22
  - Harriette Simpson Arnow, American novelist (b. 1908)
  - Martin Harlinghausen, German air force general (b. 1902)
  - Charles Starrett, American actor (b. 1903)
- March 23 – Moshe Feinstein, Orthodox rabbi (b. 1895)
- March 24 – Krzysztof Mikołaj Radziwiłł, Polish translator and politician (b. 1898)
- March 28 – Virginia Gilmore, American actress (b. 1919)
- March 29 – Harry Ritz, American actor (b. 1907)
- March 30 – James Cagney, American actor (b. 1899)
- March 31
  - O'Kelly Isley, American singer of The Isley Brothers (b. 1937)
  - Jerry Paris, American actor and director (b. 1925)

April

Mircea Eliade

The Duchess of Windsor

- April 3 – Peter Pears, English tenor (b. 1910)
- April 7 – Leonid Kantorovich, Russian economist, Nobel Prize laureate (b. 1912)
- April 8 – Yukiko Okada, Japanese idol singer (b. 1967)
- April 13 – Stephen Stucker, American actor (b. 1947)
- April 14 – Simone de Beauvoir, French feminist writer (b. 1908)
- April 15
  - Jean Genet, French writer (b. 1910)
  - Tim McIntire, American actor (b. 1944)
- April 17 – Marcel Dassault, French aircraft industrialist (b. 1892)
- April 19

- o Aileen Britton, Australian actress (b. 1916)
- o Alvin Childress, American actor (b. 1907)
- April 22 – Mircea Eliade, Romanian historian of religions and writer (b. 1907)
- April 23
  - o Harold Arlen, American music composer (b. 1905)
  - o Jim Laker, English cricketer (b. 1922)
  - o Otto Preminger, Austrian-born film director (b. 1906)
- April 24 – The Duchess of Windsor (the former Wallis Simpson), widow of the late Duke of Windsor (formerly Edward VIII) (b. 1896)
- April 26
  - o Broderick Crawford, American actor (b. 1911)
  - o Bessie Love, American actress (b. 1898)
  - o Lou van Burg Dutch television personality and game show host (b. 1917)
  - o Dechko Uzunov, Bulgarian painter (b. 1899)
- April 30 – Robert Stevenson, English film director (b. 1905)

May

Robert Alda

- May 1 – Hylda Baker, English comedy actress (b. 1905)
- May 2 – Henri Toivonen, Finnish rally car driver (b. 1956)
- May 3 – Robert Alda, American-born actor (b. 1914)

- May 9
  - Herschel Bernardi, American actor (b. 1923)
  - Tenzing Norgay, Nepalese sherpa (b. 1914)
- May 11
  - Henry Plumer McIlhenny, American art collector, socialite, philanthropist and the chairman of the Philadelphia Art Museum (b. 1910)
  - Fritz Pollard, American football player and member of the Pro Football Hall of Fame (b. 1894)
- May 12
  - Elisabeth Bergner, Austrian actress (b. 1897)
  - Alicia Moreau de Justo, Argentine physician, politician, pacifist and human rights activist (b. 1885)
- May 14 – Janne Aikala, Finnish murder victim (b. 1975)
- May 15
  - Elio de Angelis, Italian race car driver (b. 1958)
  - Theodore White, American writer (b. 1915)
- May 19 – Jimmy Lyons, American musician (b. 1931)
- May 23
  - Altiero Spinelli, Italian political theorist and European federalist (b. 1907)
  - Sterling Hayden, American actor (b. 1916)
- May 24
  - Robert Holmes, British scriptwriter (b. 1926)
  - Yakima Canutt, American actor and stuntman (b. 1895)
- May 25 – Chester Bowles, American politician (b. 1901)
- May 26 – Gian-Carlo Coppola, American film producer (b. 1963)
- May 27 – Ajoy Mukherjee, Indian politician, Chief Minister of West Bengal (b. 1901)

- May 30 – Perry Ellis, American fashion designer (b. 1940)
- May 31
    - Jane Frank, American artist (b. 1918)
    - James Rainwater, American physicist, Nobel Prize laureate (b. 1917)

June

Benny Goodman

- June 3 – Anna Neagle, English actress (b. 1904)
- June 5 – Bryan Grant, American tennis champion (b. 1909)
- June 6 – William Joynt, officer, farm labourer (b. 1889)
- June 11 – Chesley Bonestell, American painter (b. 1888)
- June 13
    - Benny Goodman, American jazz musician (b. 1909)
    - Ulla Strömstedt, Swedish actress (b. 1939)
- June 14
    - Jorge Luis Borges, Argentine writer (b. 1899)
    - Alan Jay Lerner, American lyricist (b. 1918)
    - Marlin Perkins, American zoologist (b. 1905)
- June 16 – Maurice Duruflé, French composer (b. 1902)
- June 17 – Kate Smith, American singer (b. 1907)
- June 18 – Frances Scott Fitzgerald, daughter of F. Scott Fitzgerald and Zelda Sayre (b. 1921)
- June 19

- Len Bias, American basketball player (b. 1963)
- Coluche, stage name of Michel Colucci, French comedian and humorist (b. 1944)
- June 21 – Assi Rahbani, Lebanese composer, musician, conductor and author (b. 1923)
- June 27 – Don Rogers, American football player (b. 1962)
- June 29
  - Jack Christiansen, American football player (Detroit Lions) and member of the Pro Football Hall of Fame (b. 1928)
  - Robert Drivas, American actor (b. 1938)

July

Oscar Zariski

Fritz Albert Lipmann

- July 3 – Rudy Vallée, American singer, actor, and bandleader (b. 1901)

- July 4 – Oscar Zariski, Russian mathematician (b. 1899)
- July 6 – Jagjivan Ram, Indian politician (b. 1908)
- July 8
  - Hyman G. Rickover, American admiral (b. 1900)
  - Skeeter Webb, baseball player (b. 1909)
- July 12 – Wacław Kisielewski, Polish pianist (b. 1943)
- July 14
  - Raymond Loewy, French-born industrial designer (b. 1893)
  - Joseph Vogt, German classical historian (b. 1895)
- July 15
  - Florence Halop, American actress (b. 1923)
  - Billy Haughton, American harness driver and trainer (b. 1923)
- July 19 – Alfredo Binda, Italian cyclist (b. 1902)
- July 21 – Ernest Maas, American screenwriter (b. 1892)
- July 22 – Ede Staal, Dutch singer-songwriter (b. 1941)
- July 24
  - Fritz Albert Lipmann, American biochemist, recipient of the Nobel Prize in Physiology or Medicine (b. 1899)
  - Laurie Nash, Australian sportsman (b. 1910)
  - Yoshiyuki Tsuruta, Japanese Olympic swimmer (b. 1903)
- July 25
  - Ted Lyons, American baseball player (Chicago White Sox) and member of the MLB Hall of Fame (b. 1900)
  - Vincente Minnelli, American film director (b. 1903)
- July 26 – W. Averell Harriman, American diplomat and politician (b. 1891)
- July 27 – Osbert Lancaster, British cartoonist (b. 1908)

- July 31 – Teddy Wilson, American jazz pianist (b. 1912)

August

- August 1 – Ignatius Joseph Kasimo Hendrowahyono, Indonesian politician (b. 1900)
- August 2 – Renato Leduc, Mexican poet and journalist (b. 1897)
- August 4 – Willem Ruis, Dutch game show host (b. 1945)
- August 10 – Chuck McKinley, American tennis champion (b. 1941)
- August 16 – Jaime Sáenz, Bolivian poet, novelist, and short story writer (b. 1921)
- August 19
  - Hermione Baddeley, English actress (b. 1906)
  - Charles Radoff, Russian painter (b. 1894)
  - Lorenzo Tucker, American actor (b. 1907)
- August 20 – Milton Acorn, Canadian poet, writer, and playwright (b. 1923)
- August 21 – Thad Jones, American jazz musician (b. 1923)
- August 22 – Celâl Bayar, ex-President of Turkey (b. 1883)
- August 26 – Ted Knight, American actor (b. 1923)
- August 27 – George Nepia, New Zealand Maori rugby player (b. 1905)
- August 29 – Arthur Meyerhoff, American advertising agency executive and entrepreneur (b. 1895)
- August 30 – George Pelawa, American ice hockey star Minnesota Mr. Hockey (b. 1968)
- August 31
  - Urho Kekkonen, President of Finland (b. 1900)

- Henry Moore, British sculptor (b. 1898)

September

- September 1
    - Earl B. Dickerson, prominent African American attorney (b. 1891)
    - Murray Hamilton, American actor (b. 1923)
- September 4 – Hank Greenberg, Jewish-American baseball player (Detroit Tigers) and member of the MLB Hall of Fame (b. 1911)
- September 6 – Blanche Sweet, American actress (b. 1896)
- September 7 – Omar Ali Saifuddien III, Sultan of Brunei (b. 1914)
- September 11
    - Jacques Henri Lartigue, French painter (b. 1894)
    - Henry DeWolf Smyth, American physicist (b. 1898)
- September 12 – Frank Nelson, American actor (b. 1911)
- September 18 – Pat Phoenix, British actress (b. 1923)
- September 21 – Cheryl Keeton, American murder victim (b. 1949)
- September 22 – József Asbóth, Hungarian tennis champion (b. 1917)
- September 23 – Gottfried Freiherr von Banfield, Austro-Hungarian naval aeroplane pilot in the First World War (b. 1890)
- September 25 – Nikolay Semyonov, Russian chemist, Nobel Prize laureate (b. 1896)
- September 26 – Noboru Terada, Japanese Olympic swimmer (b. 1917)

- September 27 – Cliff Burton, American bassist (Metallica) (b. 1962)
- September 28 – Robert Helpmann, Australian dancer and choreographer (b. 1909)
- September 29 – Prince George Valdemar of Denmark (b. 1920)
- September 30 – Storm Jameson, English journalist and author (b. 1891)

October

Samora Machel

Albert Szent-Györgyi

- October 5
  - Hal B. Wallis, American film producer (b. 1898)

- ○ James H. Wilkinson, English mathematician (b. 1919)
- October 7 – Wallace Wade, American football coach, University of Alabama, Duke University (b. 1892)
- October 11 – Boris Leven, Russian-born art director (b. 1908)
- October 14 – Keenan Wynn, American actor (b. 1916)
- October 15 – Jerry Smith, American football All Pro tight end, Washington Redskins, NFL (b. 1943)
- October 16 – Arthur Grumiaux, Belgian violinist (b. 1921)
- October 19 – Samora Machel, President of Mozambique (b. 1933)
- October 22 – Albert Szent-Györgyi, Hungarian physiologist, Nobel Prize laureate (b. 1893)
- October 23 – Edward Adelbert Doisy, American biochemist, recipient of the Nobel Prize in Physiology or Medicine (b. 1893)
- October 25 – Forrest Tucker, American actor (*F Troop*) (b. 1919)
- October 26 – Jackson Scholz, American runner (b. 1897)
- October 28 – Ian Marter, British actor and writer (b. 1944)
- October 31 – Robert S. Mulliken, American physicist and chemist, recipient of the Nobel Prize in Chemistry (b. 1896)

November

Cary Grant

- November 2 – Paul Frees, American voice actor (b. 1920)
- November 5 – Claude Jutra, Canadian film director (b. 1930)
- November 6 – Elisabeth Grümmer, Alsatian soprano (b. 1911)
- November 8
    - Artur London, Czech statesman (b. 1915)
    - Vyacheslav Molotov, Soviet politician (b. 1890)
- November 10 – Rogelio de la Rosa, Filipino actor and politician (b. 1916)
- November 11 – Roger C. Carmel, American actor (b. 1932)
- November 15 – Alexandre Tansman, French composer and virtuoso pianist (b. 1897)
- November 16 – Siobhán McKenna, Irish actress (b. 1923)
- November 18 – Gia Carangi, American supermodel (b. 1960)
- November 21
    - Jerry Colonna, American comedian (b. 1904)
    - Dar Robinson, American film stuntman (b. 1947)
- November 22
    - Scatman Crothers, American actor, musician (b. 1910)

- William Bradford Huie, American journalist, editor, publisher and author (b. 1910)
- November 25 – Ivan Magill, Irish-born anaesthetist (b. 1888)
- November 29 – Cary Grant, British actor (b. 1904)

December

Harold Macmillan

- December 1 – Bobby Layne, American football player (Detroit Lions) and member of the Pro Football Hall of Fame (b. 1926)
- December 2 – Desi Arnaz, Cuban-born actor (b. 1917)
- December 3 – Austin Hayes, Irish footballer (b. 1958)
- December 10 – Susan Cabot, American actress (b. 1927)
- December 12 – Paul Verner, German politician (b. 1911)
- December 13 – Heather Angel, English actress (b. 1909)
- December 15 – Serge Lifar, Russian dancer and choreographer (b. 1905)
- December 16 – John Nathaniel Couch, American mycologist (b. 1896)
- December 17 – Guillermo Cano Isaza, Colombian journalist (b. 1925)

- December 18 – Andrew Tsu, Chinese Anglican bishop (b. 1885)
- December 21 – Willy Coppens, Belgian pilot (b. 1892)
- December 22 – Ida Cook (aka Mary Burchell), British novelist and campaigner for Jewish refugees (b. 1904)
- December 26 – Elsa Lanchester, English actress (b. 1902)
- December 28 – Jan Nieuwenhuys, Dutch painter (b. 1922)
- December 29
    - Harold Macmillan, 1st Earl of Stockton, Prime Minister of the United Kingdom 1957–1963 (b. 1894)
    - Andrei Tarkovsky, Russian film director (b. 1932)
- December 31 – Lloyd Haynes, American actor (b. 1934)

Date unknown

- Hilda Conkling, child poet (b. 1910)
- Iren Marik, classical Hungarian pianist (b. 1906)
- Felix Tikotin, architect and art collector (b. 1893)

Nobel Prizes

- Physics – Ernst Ruska, Gerd Binnig, Heinrich Rohrer
- Chemistry – Dudley R. Herschbach, Yuan T. Lee, John Charles Polanyi
- Physiology or Medicine – Stanley Cohen, Rita Levi-Montalcini
- Literature – Wole Soyinka
- Peace – Elie Wiesel
- Economics – James Buchanan Jr

In the News.

Fuji introduces the disposable camera.

Comet Halley reaches the closest point to the Earth, during its second visit to the solar system in the 20th century.

The Space Shuttle Challenger disintegrates 73 seconds after launching, killing all seven astronauts on board.

Mike Tyson becomes the youngest Heavyweight Champion in history

The Soviet Union launches the Mir space station

Chernobyl disaster

Mexico football World Cup begins – Mexico 86, Argentina beat West Germany 3-2 to win World Cup

Prince Andrew marries Sarah Ferguson at Westminster Abbey

Suzy Lamplugh disappears after a meeting in London